LITERACY IN 3[illegible]

Paulo Freire's Process in North East Brazil

Cynthia Brown

Writers and Readers Publishing Cooperative

Published by Writers and Readers Publishing Cooperative
14 Talacre Road, London NW5
Printed by Expression Printers Limited
London N1 4AZ
ISBN 0 904613 05 4

CONTENTS

INTRODUCTION

The writer of this pamphlet, Cynthia Brown, is one of the teachers at the Centre for Open Learning and Teaching, Inc., a non-profit corporation established in 1972 in Berkeley, California. Its Board of Directors consists of five people elected annually: in 1974-75 the directors are Brenda Bay, Cynthia Brown, Maria Rose Grunwaldt, Herbert Kohl and Ray Nitta. The Centre tries to analyze and act within public schools to achieve non-racist and non-authoritarian environments where children can learn in natural ways and where the hopes of all the parents in the community can be realized.

Specifically, the Centre has over three years developed three related programmes. One is an elementary credential programme, in conjunction with the University Without Walls, Berkeley, in which people can complete the fifth year of their training to become teachers. At the end of this year's supervised work in classrooms, workshops and seminars, these people are eligible to receive a California elementary teaching credential. In three years, forty people have received credentials through the Centre's programme.

As part of the credential programme, the Centre operates a Curriculum Centre full-time in a bungalow of a public elementary school. This Curriculum Centre is equipped with the basic tools and materials so that students and teachers can learn to create their own materials for their classrooms. A continuous programme of workshops is offered at the Curriculum Centre, on topics such as maths games, bookmaking, metric activities, making and playing games of many cultures. These workshops are open to all parents and teachers as well as to student teachers.

The third aspect of the Centre's work has been the development of multi-cultural curriculum materials, especially books and games. With a grant from the Dolores Kohl Educational Foundation, the Centre has developed three bi-lingual books for Spanish-speaking children beginning to read - or for any children. Ray Nitta, who coordinates the Curriculum Centre, has designed and installed several game centres in elementary classrooms. He and others have been exploring ways to teach young children traditional games from many cultures, such as Dozo and Wari. The Centre plans to open a larger workshop and expand its curriculum materials in the year ahead.

LITERACY IN 30 HOURS: PAULO FREIRE'S PROCESS IN NORTHEAST BRAZIL

by Cynthia Brown

Learning to read is a political act. In a literate society being able to read is a necessary step toward making decisions and sharing power. A nonliterate person may be very powerful within a nonliterate subculture, but within the dominant culture a nonreader is marginal. She/he cannot fill out tests and applications, cannot determine what is in contracts without a trusted adviser who can read, has no access to information controlled by professionals, and often is denied the right to vote. Learning to read gives access to information, protection against fraud, and participation as a citizen.

Learning to read is a step toward political participation. But how people exercise their ability to read reflects in part the political attitudes of their teachers. If nonreaders learn to read by writing and reading their own words and opinions, then they learn that their perceptions of reality are valid to others and can influence even those in authority. If, on the other hand, their teachers require them to learn the words and ideas in a primer which is donated by those in power, then the learners must accept that experience as more valid than their own. They must accept the concepts of social and economic structure transmitted by the teacher - or decide not to learn to read.

By understanding the political dimensions of reading, Paulo Freire developed materials that enabled adults to learn to read in 30 to 40 hours. Freire was born and lived until 1964 in Recife, on the northeast coast of Brazil. In 1960, Recife had 80,000 children from 7 to 14 years old who did not attend school. Adult illiteracy was estimated at 60 to 70 percent. Crusades against illiteracy had been waged repeatedly without much effect. But Freire believed that adults could learn to read rapidly if reading were not part of a cultural imposition on them. After all, adults speak an extraordinarily rich and complex language which they could set down graphically if only they were given the tools to do so.

For more than 15 years Freire had accumulated experience in adult education. In 1959, he received a PhD degree from the University of Recife and stayed at the university as a teacher of philosophy and education. He envisioned the university as a base for the education of all people, not merely for the rich and the educated. While teaching there he coordinated the Adult Education Programme of the Popular Culture Movement, which set up circles of culture in slum areas and encouraged popular festivals and performances. In February 1962, Freire became director of the university's newly established Cultural Extension Service.

The political realities of early 1962 supported Freire's hope that the Cultural Extension Service could be a resource for all the people. In October 1962, a coalition of the Socialist, Labour, and Communist parties elected the mayor of Recife, Miguel Arraes, to the state governorship. Arraes appointed the founder of the Popular Culture Movement, Germano Coelho, to be state secretary of education. As the Cultural Extension Service developed its literacy programme, it received financial assistance from the United States Agency for International Development (USAID) - enough to run a pilot project and to train 70 people in the use of the materials. USAID terminated its assistance in January 1964.

By that time the upper class and the small middle class in Brazil had become frightened by signs of growing political awareness among the masses. On April 1, 1964, the military leaders of Brazil took control of the government at all levels. Freire was under house arrest until June, imprisoned for 70 days, and finally sought refuge in Chile. After a year in Santiago he spent a year in Cambridge, Massachusetts, and in February 1970, he went to Geneva, Switzerland, to work for the World Council of Churches.

In the circles of culture set up by the Popular Culture Movement, Freire and his colleagues arranged discussions of such topics as nationalism, development, illiteracy, democracy. They introduced these topics with pictures or slides, then led a dialogue in which they exchanged points of view with nonliterates. Amazed by the results, Freire became ever more convinced that for adults, learning to read should be a process of analyzing reality, that adults can become critically conscious of their situation, and that when this occurs enormous energy is available for learning to read.

Yet Freire and his teams found many Brazilian nonliterates so submerged in their daily struggles that they had no awareness of whether or how they could change their lives in any way. They resisted being told they had problems. They believed that the conditions of their lives were due to God's will or to fate. In order to change this passive attitude Freire introduced the anthropological concept of culture, that is, the distinction between nature and culture. Freire believed that discussing this distinction would lead nonliterates to the discovery that they are makers of culture as much as literate people are, that aspects of their lives are man-made and therefore subject to change. The distinction between nature and culture included for Freire the difference between men and other animals and the importance of oral and written language in that difference.

Freire asked his friend, the well-known artist Francisco Brennand, to draw a series of pictures that could be used to stimulate discussions about nature and culture, men and animals, and culture in the lives of people. Brennand painted a series of 10 pictures. Eight appear below, made from slides in Freire's possession. The originals were taken from him. To complete the series two pictures are included from a later version of the series drawn by Vicente de Abreu and published in Paulo Freire's *Education for Critical Consciousness.*

This sequence of 10 pictures is tightly analyzed and structured. The first picture (Figure 1) is carefully designed to elicit an initial distinction between culture and nature, while succeeding pictures are sequenced to draw out various subtleties of the distinction, namely: the difference between man and other animals being man's culture-making and communicating capacities (Figures 2-5); nature transformed into culture by man's work (Figures 3, 6, 7); communications as culture (Figures 2, 8); and patterns of behaviour and traditions as culture (Figure 9). The final picture (Figure 10) challenges the group to analyze its own behaviour - the most distinctive capacity of people.

Figure 1 provides a familiar image from which a nonliterate from north-eastern Brazil can use his knowledge to distinguish between nature and culture. The coordinator begins the discussion with the question: "What do you see in the picture?" This naming of the objects is important because people not accustomed to graphic representation may not easily identify what is meant to be shown. Notice that Brennand painted the pictures in one dimension without the conventions used by schooled artists for showing perspective. The coordinator then leads the discussion into the distinction between nature and culture by asking questions like: "Who made the well?" "Why did he do it?" "What materials did he use?" The questions continued: "Who made the tree?" "How is the tree different from the well?" "Who made the pig, the birds, the man?" "Who made the house, the hoe, the book?" Gradually the discussion moves to the conclusion that people use natural materials to change their situation, to create culture. Nonliterates know this distinction, but the discussion gives them the words to name and clarify it. At the conclusion of this discussion participants are already conscious of being cultured.

The second discussion, provoked by Figure 2, concerns the relationship among people. People can make culture while animals

A BOMBA

A TERRIVEL BOMBA ATÔMICA
E A RADIO-ATIVIDADE
SIGNIFICAM TERROR
RUINA E CALAMIDADE

SE ACABASSEM COM A GUERRA
E TUDO FICASSE UNIDO
O NOSSO MUNDO DE HOJE
NÃO SERIA DESTRUIDO

cannot, and people, unlike animals, can communicate extensively with each other, both orally and graphically. Nature mediates the relationships and communications of people. The natural world is real and can be known by investigation and dialogue; human disagreements can be checked against the natural reality. The proper relationship among people is discussed as being that of subjects communicating with each other, not as objects being used by anyone. This communication must take place as dialogue between equals, with the perception of each person having equal validity. If one person assumes a superior position to another, he issues communiques instead of communicating, and the dialogue is broken.

The next three discussions (Figures 3, 4, 5) refine the concept of culture and raise the question of how culture is transmitted to younger generations. The group is asked to name what represents culture in Figure 3. Characteristically, the group mentions the bow and arrow and the feathers. When asked if the feathers do not belong to nature, they answer that feathers belong to nature when on the bird, but people change them into culture by making clothing of them. The Indian teaches his skills to his son by direct experience, without writing, and the group discovers that those unable to read and write belong to a nonliterate culture like that of the Indian, even if they are part of a literate culture such as that shown in Figure 4. Here the hunter is using a tool so complex in its construction that directions for making it must be recorded, and only those who can read can learn to make it. Moreover, in this culture only those who can read can earn enough money to buy guns, so access to their use is controlled by the literate members of this culture. Participants discuss the technological advance represented by the rifle compared with the bow and arrow, and they analyze this hunter's growing possibilities for transforming the world. This transformation makes sense only to the degree that it liberates and humanizes people. Finally, the group discusses the implication of education for technological development.

Figure 5 reinforces man's culture-making capacity by showing a cat who cannot make tools to extend his hunting capabilities. A nonliterate from Brasilia pointed out: "Of these three, only two are hunters - the two men. They are hunters because they made culture first and then hunted. The third, the cat, who did not make culture either before or after the hunt, is not a hunter (*cacador*). He is a pursuer (*persequidor*)." The series of the three hunters always provoked many observations by the participants about people and animals, and about such things as instinct, intelligence, liberty, and education.

After this somewhat general discussion of culture referring to other places (countryside) and times (Indian preliterate culture), Figure 6 ensures that participants in a circle of culture discover themselves as makers of culture. Here they see their brothers from the people making clay pots, and they realize that clay pots are as much culture as the work of a great sculptor. "I make shoes," said one participant, "and now I discover that I have as much value as a professor who makes books."

Figure 7 shows the use to which someone has put a clay pot. Here not only is clay transformed into culture, but flowers, which in the field are part of nature, have been changed into culture by the person who arranged them. "I make culture. I know how to do that," recognized a woman, very moved, in a circle of culture in Recife. A graphic signal is introduced for the first time in this picture. The flowers in the vase are represented by a drawing of them on the clay of the vase. Nature, transformed into culture, has been transformed once again into a written symbol.

Figure 8 is the next step in graphic representation. It shows that words known by and put together by nonliterates can be written down and are as much poetry as poems by educated people. This poem is a popular song, part of an elaborate tradition among nonliterates in northeast Brazil whereby the news is spread from town to town by singers. These singers play guitars and sing in pairs, each challenging the other to invent another verse incorporating the latest news. This picture is highly exciting to nonliterates because it shows them that they can learn to read the words and songs they already know.

Figure 9 shows two cowboys, one from the south of Brazil who is dressed in wool and the other from the northeast who is dressed in leather. This scene is designed to expand the idea of culture by showing that clothes and ways of behaving are also part of culture. The discussion focuses on the clothes of the cowboys. The southern cowboy makes his clothes of wool because sheep are available and wool keeps him warm. The northeastern cowboy uses leather because cows are available and leather is tough enough to protect him against cacti and scrubs. By discussing the cowboys' clothing and why it is different, participants realize that patterns of behaving are created by people in response to necessity. Sometimes this picture leads to a discussion of people's resistance to change - that traditions, such as clothing, develop out of necessity, but the necessity may pass while the tradition stays.

Figure 10 enables the group to develop its critical consciousness

- to look at itself and reflect on its own activity. This picture shows a circle of culture functioning; participants can easily identify it as representing themselves. The coordinator introduces the phrase "democratization of culture" to be discussed in the light of what has been happening in the circle of culture. As one participant concluded: "The democratization of culture has to do with what we are and with what we make as people. Not with what they think and want for us." The function of the circle of culture is examined by everyone - what the experience has meant, what dialogue is, and what it means to raise one's consciousness. By the time the group had reached this tenth picture, participants had regained enormous confidence in themselves, pride in their culture, and desire to learn to read.

The coordinators conduct the discussion of the 10 situations orally without using any kind of text or written representation. The fact that participants could not read was not allowed to prevent their considering highly complex issues. Since they could not read, ideas were introduced in the graphic representation they could understand - pictures. Because the participants were given a chance to express their real knowledge and were not demeaned by their inability to read, they were able to recover their eagerness for learning to read.

Freire called the process just described *conscientização*, usually translated as "conscientization." For him conscientization is a process in which people are encouraged to analyze their reality, to become more aware of the constraints on their lives, and to take action to transform their situation. For Freire education is either liberating or domesticating, teaching people either to be critical and free of constraints or to accept things as they are. If literacy is not to be domesticating, Freire believed, then it must be part of a process of conscientization. [2]

Freire and his colleagues developed the linguistic materials for their literacy programme from two premises: (1) Adults can learn to read with ease words that are highly familiar and meaningful to them. (2) It ought to be possible to select a brief list of words that would contain all the phonemes in Portuguese, so that learning this minimal linguistic universe would enable a reader to sound out any other words or to record any words he knew orally. (This premise appeared possible because Portuguese is for the

2 No verbatim record from Freire's circles is available, but the process of conscientization is clearly illustrated in the account of Stokely Carmichael's speech class, held for field workers of the Student Nonviolent Coordinating Committee in 1965, reprinted in Miriam Wasserman, ed., *Demystifying School* (New York: Praeger, 1974), pp. 327-330.

most part a phonetic, syllabic language.)

In order to prepare for teaching reading in any specific community, Freire's teams visited the community to investigate its culture. They explained why they had come and solicited help from volunteers from the community, whom they called co-investigators. Together they examined all the familiar activities of the community, cross-checking their perceptions and analyzing the significant words used by the community. From these lists of words they developed a short list of words chosen by a double criterion: (1) a word's emotional impact and capacity for provoking discussion, and (2) its phonemic value in presenting all the sounds of Portuguese. Freire and his colleagues observed, both in Brazil and in Chile, that no more than 17 words are necessary for teaching adults to read and write syllabic, phonetic languages such as Portuguese and Spanish. They called these words "generative," in the double sense that the words could generate among non-literates impassioned discussions of the social and political realities of their lives (in Freire's words, they could engage the learners in "problematizing their existential situations"), and by breaking the 17 words into syllables and rearranging the syllables non-literates could generate other words and transcribe their own words.

After choosing 16 or 17 generative words Freire and his colleagues found they must analyze carefully the sequence in which to present the words. Three principles guided their order of presentation. First, the initial word must be trisyllabic, such that each of the three syllables consists of one consonant and one vowel. Second, less common and more difficult phonetic material should appear toward the end of the list. For example, words with "x", "z", "q", and "ao" tend to appear late on the list. Third, words that name concrete and familiar objects should appear early, while words naming more abstract social and political realities should appear later on the list. These principles can be seen in the word lists (Lists 1-4) used by Freire or by teams using his process.

Freire believed the ideas represented by the words must be critically discussed before the words themselves were analyzed as graphic symbols. So his teams prepared a picture to illustrate each word. For example, for the word *tijolo* (brick) a picture of a construction scene was prepared. This picture was shown first without the word *tijolo*. Only after the group had discussed building with bricks, their own houses, housing as a community problem, obstacles to better housing, and whatever other topics were generated, was the second picture introduced showing the construction scene together with the word *tijolo*. In the third picture or slide the word *tijolo* appeared alone. In the same manner pictures were prepared for each of the 16 words in order to ensure full discussion of the significance of the words before any linguistic or graphic analysis was made.

On every word list the first word has three syllables. The reason for this is that one of Freire's colleagues discovered that a chart could be made of the syllables of trisyllabic words in a way that helped nonliterates grasp the structure of Portuguese words. For

List 1

Used in Cajueiro Sêco, a slum in Recife

tijolo	brick
voto	vote
siri	crab
palha	straw
biscate	odd job
cinza	ashes
doença	illness
chafariz	fountain
máquina	machine (sewing)
emprêgo	employment
engenho	sugar mill
mangue	swamp
terra	land, soil
enxada	hoe
classe	class

List 2

Used in Tiriri, an agricultural colony in the city of Cabo

tijolo	brick
voto	vote
roçado	manioc field
abacaxí	pineapple
cacimba	well
passa	raisin
feira	market
milho	corn flour
maniva	kind of manioc
planta	plant
lombriga	roundworm
engenho	sugar mill
guia	guide (for a blind person)
barracão	small store rooms near market place
charque	dried meat
cozinha sal	kitchen salt

List 3

Used in Maceio, a city on the sea

tijolo	brick
voto	vote
casamento	wedding
carroça	cart
peixe	fish
jangada	fishing boat
balança	scale for weighing fish
Brasil	Brazil
máquina	machine (sewing)
farinha	flour
coco	coconut
fome	hunger
comida	food
sindicato	union
trabalho	work
limpeza	cleanliness

List 4

Used in the state of Rio, a rural area and satellite of the city of Rio de Janeiro

favela	slum
chuva	rain
arado	plow
terreno	plot of land
comida	food
batuque	popular dance with African rhythms
poço	well
bicicleta	bicycle
trabalho	work
salário	salary
profissão	profession
govêrno	government
mangue	swamp
engenho	sugar mill
enrada	hoe
tijolo	brick
riqueza	riches, wealth

example, after introducing *tijolo* the coordinator broke the word into syllables. After reading aloud the individual syllables with the group, the coordinator presented the first one, "ti," like this "ta te ti to tu." At first the group recognized only "ti," but by reading these five syllables aloud they learned that the "t" sound was constant and they learned the sound of the five vowels. Next, "jo" was introduced in the same manner, "ja je ji jo ju," and was followed by "la le li lo lu." Finally, these three presentations were combined in a chart, called the "card of discovery":

ta	te	ti	to	tu
ja	je	ji	jo	ju
la	le	li	lo	lu

After one horizontal reading and one vertical reading, the coordinator asked the group to put together other words by combining the syllables on the chart in different ways. Often the group began to do this with no suggestion. For example, they might recognize *luta* (struggle) or *loja* (store). Other possibilities are: *tatu* (armadillo), *jato* (jet), *lula* (squid), *lote* (lot), *talo* (stalk), *lata* (tin can), and *tule* (tulle). Sometimes they combined syllables in ways that were not actual words, which did not matter so long as they discovered the mechanism of combining syllables. Coordinators were trained to accept any combination of syllables and to let the group discuss which words were actual ones.

In the state of Rio Grande do Norte a group called combinations of syllables that were actual words "thinking words" (*palavras do pensamento*) and others "dead words" (*palavras mortas*). In a circle of culture in Angicos, Rio Grande do Norte, one of the participants went to the blackboard on the fifth night of meetings to write, he said, a "thinking word." Easily he wrote: *o povo vai resouver os poblemas do Brasil votando conciente* ("the people will solve the problems of Brazil by informed voting").[3]

It is important to notice that Freire and his colleagues chose not to use books, or primers, as the format for their programme. Instead they used large posters, filmstrips, or slides. They found Polish slide projectors available at about $13 each, and they used the whitewashed stucco walls common to community buildings for screens. They avoided primers on the grounds that they are

3 This may be compared with accepted literate Brazilian Portuguese: *O povo vai resolver os problemas do Brasil, votando consciente.* Of the three variations, two are due to the fact that Portuguese is not perfectly phonetic, i.e., the "l" in *resolver* sounds like "u", and "c" records the "s" sound in *consciente* without requiring the "s". The third variation is a difference in speech; the man from Angicos says *poblemas* rather than *problemas.*

mechanical and do not lend themselves to much flexibility in discussion. Furthermore, primers discourage people from expressing and writing their own ideas and words. The generation of words, the decision about which formations are actual words, the use of the words, and the messages that the words should convey - all these decisions should be they believed, jointly undertaken by nonliterate adults and the coordinators of the discussions.

Two colleagues of Freire's in the Popular Culture Movement felt differently about this issue and wrote a *Primer for Adults.* In this primer five words - *povo* (people), *voto* (vote), *vida* (life), *saúde* (health), and *pão* (bread) - are introduced, broken into syllables, and varied in the style used by Freire's teams. The first sentence reads: *O voto é do povo* ("The vote belongs to the people") The words and messages continue: "People without a house live in shacks." Then the final word "peace" and its messages "The Northeast will only have peace when the roots of its ills have been eradicated." "Peace grows out of justice."[4]

This primer is extraordinarily better than the usual ones. Anisio Teixeira, the director of the Brazilian National Institute of Pedagogical Studies, said of it in 1962:

> "This book effectively teaches reading as if the northeastern non-literate were introducing his own life. The words, the sentences, the phrases are those that would inevitably occur to the non-literate if he himself were writing his own primer . . . Learning to read ought to be a simple transposition of one's actual oral language to a written language. This has been realized to an unprecedented extent in the *Primer for Adults* . . . Those who consider it subversive must consider life and truth subversive and deceit and nonsense orderly."[5]

But the very excellence of this primer reveals the basic difficulties of primers as a format: the phonetic variation becomes tedious and the messages are not the direct opinions of the learners. Because the ideas are those of the teachers, the book is an instrument of propaganda; in supposing what nonliterates may believe, it tells them what they should believe. As long as the message is donated, it domesticates those who accept it to the uncritical acceptance of whatever teachers and writers say should be believed.

4 This primer was written by Josina Maria Lopes de Godoy and Norma Porto Carreiro Coelho. I was given a copy in 1965 by officials of USAID in Recife. The military confiscated all known copies, but USAID saved one to show how communistic the area had been before the takeover.

5 From an interview with Dr. Teixeira reprinted in the *Revista Brasileira de Estudos Pedagogicos* XXXVIII, 88 (October-December 1962), pp. 158-159.

APPLYING FREIRE'S PROCESS

To summarize a bit, the following preparations were made by Freire and his colleagues before convening a meeting of nonliterates to be taught.

1. Acceptance by the political authorities of the necessary conditions was sought. Freire's requirements of mayors and governors were: no partisan interference, technical independence, and acknowledgement that the education provided would cause an internal and external liberation of the people.
2. The life and vocabulary of the community were investigated.
3. The 16 or so generative words were "codified," that is, a poster, slide, or filmstrip of the local situation described by each of the chosen words was prepared.
4. A card of discovery for the initial word was formulated.
5. A place to meet - a church, school, or whatever community building was available - was arranged.
6. Coordinators, not teachers, for each group were selected and trained. This was a major problem in setting up the programme. The technical aspect of the procedure was not difficult to impart, but the creation of a new attitude required a period of supervision to help coordinators avoid the temptation of "anti-dialogue."
7. A circle of culture, not a school or class, was organized consisting of 25 to 30 nonliterates who would be participants, not pupils.

Once the groups convened the procedure went as follows:

1. Meetings were held every week-night for one hour during six to eight weeks.
2. The first two to eight sessions were devoted to analyzing the 10 pictures illustrating the distinction between nature and culture.
3. At the next session the first generative word was introduced, as described above. At the end of this session participants were asked to make up more words from the card of discovery and to bring their lists to the next meeting.
4. At the remaining sessions the other 16 or so generative words were introduced one at a time. Participants practised writing and reading aloud, they expressed opinions and wrote them down, they examined newspapers and discussed local issues.

Those who finished the literacy course, perhaps three-quarters of those who began, could read and write simple texts, make something of the local newspapers, and discuss Brazilian problems. On one occasion a woman in a circle of culture in Rio Grande do Norte read aloud a telegram in a newspaper as an exercise. The telegram discussed the exploitation of salt in Rio Grade do Norte. A visitor to the circle asked the woman, "Lady, do you know what exploitation means?" "Perhaps you, a rich young man, don't know," she replied. "But I, a poor woman, I know what exploitation is."

It was most important to Freire that the discussions of problems did not lead to demagogical solutions. The woman who spoke of exploitation did so not with hatred but with a legitimate determination to overcome conditions that seemed to her and to all the participants highly subversive to the interest of the people.

Another participant in Rio Grande do Norte discussed the fact that he and his comrades knew how to "brand" (*ferrar*) their names. When asked by a guest what it meant to brand their names, he explained: "It means to copy our name, which the landlord writes on a paper, until we get tired, and the landlord keeps saying more! more! until we learn it by heart. Then we have to brand our names - the landlord gets us a voting certificate and sends us to vote for whom he wants." (Brazilian law refuses the vote to nonliterates, but at that time a person could qualify as literate merely by signing his name to an application form.) "But now," he continued, "we are going to un-brand our names, to really learn to write, and then vote for whom we want."

Freire and his colleagues were planning a postliteracy curriculum based on the investigations of Brazilian themes carried out by the circles of culture. They expected that 20,000 literacy circles would have been functioning in Brazil in 1964 if the military coup had not terminated the programme.

USING PAULO FREIRE'S IDEAS

In Berkeley, California, a number of teachers have been seriously interested in adapting Freire's ideas to our situation. We have been associated with each other through the Centre for Open Learning and Teaching. We have been teaching in the public schools of Berkeley, at the elementary levels. One of our specific goals is that every child in every class learns to read at least on a level considered acceptable for their age in such a way that their natural voice is still intact.

The 1974 school census in Berkeley lists 44.7% of the students as White, 44.1% Black, 6.2% Asian, 3.2% Chicano, 0.1% American Indian and 1.7% other. A system of bussing is used to approximate a proportionate diversity at each school. In classrooms we find an even greater diversity than the census suggests: children from interracial marriages, children from other countries, children from counter-cultures, very wealthy children and very poor ones. Many were not born in Berkeley; their families are extremely mobile. Family life is diverse; children may be living with one parent, with two, with extended families or in unrelated collective groups.

Our situation is different from Freire's in Recife, Brazil. We are teaching children, not adults, to read. We have schools to meet in, lots of equipment and supplies, nine months of time, every weekday from 9.00am until 2.30pm. In each group of 25 children we have several cultures represented; they are not all growing up in a single place - a city slum or an interior town. But to reach our goal we must analyze the same problem that Freire did: how does reading relate to the children's total lives and cultures?

The two interviews that follow are with teachers who have thought about Freire's work a great deal and have tried to adapt aspects of it in their own work. The first is with Brenda Bay, who served as director of the Intercommunal Youth Institute for a number of years. The Youth Institute is a community-based school in East Oakland which serves neighbourhood children as a day school and a group of about 25 children who live collectively at the school except on weekends. The children in this school are mostly Black and to a considerable extent share a common culture. The children living together share a total environment, often from infancy. The school depends heavily on donations and volunteers, so funds for supplies were sometimes not available.

After this experience Ms Bay taught in Berkeley public schools and for a summer directed the Early Learning Centre, a community-based public school with a day-care programme for children three to eight years old. Ms Bay is now a substitute teacher in Berkeley and teaches student teachers in the elementary credential programme of the University Without Walls-Berkeley.

AN INTERVIEW WITH BRENDA BAY

Brenda: I first thought about Freire in terms of teaching adults. What I think we have to focus on is not the specifics of his method, but the way in which he arrived at it. If we can see how he arrived at the method, then we can use that procedure to arrive at a method for teaching children, or on a broader scale to do anything. First, he was very aware of the fact that reading could be a dynamic kind of force that would open up information for people, and such information would allow them to participate in transforming the world to benefit their lives. On the other hand, he recognized that if anything, reading was a tool used by the oppressors to perpetuate that system (in terms of literacy and content of reading material). Thus in order for reading to be of benefit to the people he had to instil motivation and change the content.

It was necessary for Freire to study the people's culture because his lifestyle was somewhat different. He made a very intense investigation of what was going on, their language, the events in their life, the people's ideas, from the general to the more specific. This is why the pictures went from very general things to more specific things. I'm sure he had to spend some time thinking about pictures of everyday occurences he could use to get people to observe their lives in a more critical way and then go on to analyze the over-all situation. Perhaps something other than pictures could be used - it might be a series of experiences that people would share and then come together and talk about. It might be possible to get the same kind of results. Of course, in our society we would probably have to use something in addition to the pictures, because pictures are not spectacular kinds of things. It would have to be something that could stand out, that would just be interesting in itself.

In selecting the words, the approach to reading was to deal with the words that were valid, familiar, in the context in which they were being used. And then because of the way the language was structured Freire's teams could show all the interconnections with all the different sounds. I think what was key in the use of the words was the necessity to change the words from place to place in order to fit that particular environment.

Then the whole business of adding the political content. I hesitate to use the word. It's been used so much and in so many kinds of ways, but just adding the whole idea of reading as a tool to open up a world of knowledge, knowledge that can be used to transform the world. I think that those three things are the keys. I certainly use this approach in anything. It's not just an approach to reading, but to living in a constructive way.

I have never really taught any adults, but I have used Freire's approach with children - young children just starting to read. When I was teaching at the Institute I was able to use this kind of approach, because we didn't really have any books, nor the money to buy them with. So we had to teach reading by writing things down on paper or on the board. In this particular case the children were already motivated to read because of their environment. No one was afraid to read or thought it was something they couldn't do. So it was a matter of teaching. We picked out their names and some other words that were familiar. In this case the children were living in a collective, and there were different signs up to designate what belonged to who, like boy, girl, food and highly charged words like love, people, revolution, etc. Any word can be introduced to fairly young children if it is a charged word - love, people, things like that. Once a child is reading what was going on, and you have used the words until they are familiar and they feel they can do it, then that's when you can introduce other things - the different sounds, putting different syllables together. This is where we introduced the rhyming words because it builds the sight vocabulary fast. Then as you build with those words you can go into other words that are a little more difficult. Then you can really see not only how many words they can recognize but spell. In the beginning, especially, when they are learning it seems that spelling is really difficult. I find that act of writing and the mental process that has to take place helps children maintain the word in their mind, somehow. One thing that was interesting was that children learned to read each other's names because lots of things were labelled. And of course you were able to pick upon their vocabulary because you spent so much time with the children. It was your vocabulary, too, so their words were your words, so it really wasn't too difficult.

Cynthia: In teaching reading can you build a whole programme the way you've just described? If you have other resources, do you add other books and things, or can you teach children to read competently just based on the language that you generate out of their environment?

Brenda: I think it depends. Of course you can do it, but it depends on the environment the child is in. I mean, for example, you've got to take into consideration what kind of things they are going to be reading first. If they are going to be reading the kinds of things that are in the public school system, then I think that you would want to use the books in the classroom. When I go into a situation I check out to see what's of most interest. If it's a book that is in the classroom - well, there are some that you really just don't care for children to read the content is so poor. But most of the books in the room are okay. The way a book is structured is important for teaching beginning readers. The content is just children and children's activities, and children often are interested in it. You know, everyone has to live in his own school. So, there is no need to take it away from them. I think it depends. When you go into a situation you just have to accept it and see what's happening there. You can do political conscientization as far as exposing - making the children aware there is more life than what you see here, that we do live in a world with many people with many different things, and you have to have an appreciation and a respect for all people. That kind of thing, as far as I'm concerned, is political content.

As far as teaching reading, I'll see what book the children are interested in, and if it seems to be okay I'll use it. And I'll just build from there. I'll use the reader, and then I use rhyming words - you can make up a lot of sentences and things from rhyming words. I use that, with the writing and the reading. They read from the book, and they write the rhyming words and the sentences from the board and then read what they write. Then I bring in lots of examples of different things for children. So when we ask them to do something they've seen a lot of examples, because a lot of times it is very difficult for them to know what you're talking about. You have to let the children feel the idea is theirs.

Then I use pictures to attempt to expand their knowledge of the world. First, I give children pictures that they can deal with. After spending some time with children, I know what they are like. When I pass the pictures out to the children, I know which one I'm giving to whom. Then as we go along I give them something that they're not accustomed to, that requires more time looking at.

Cynthia: Earlier you mentioned that at the Institute the children's words were your words because you were with them so much. In Berkeley there are so many groups of children that often the teacher's words are not the kids' words; within one classroom there may be children with different words. How do you deal with that?

Brenda: When children are young, say six or seven, and they are just beginning to read and write, you'll find some of them will write in so-called non-standard English and some will not. Since there is no way I know of really explaining why it should be another way, and perhaps it really shouldn't be at that particular point in their development, I really don't deal with that too much. I don't teach standards of English, except that I try to emphasize that the purpose of writing is communication. It's like talking, but you're not there. If you leave things out, people are not going to know what's happening. I always point out that the purpose of writing is to be understood. That is the key thing, you know. So everything I would ask them to do would be around being able to get the message across. As children get older it can simply be explained to them (not simply) that there is a particular way of writing things for particular kinds of people, and we have to be aware of the places, the people, the different kinds of consequences. It just depends - the explanation would definitely depend on the group of children that I was talking to, as to just what the explanation would be. Especially in a situation where people are coming from many different kinds of ideas you have to be very, very careful because you want to, as a teacher, get across certain kinds of information and certain kinds of skills that will help the children in a constructive way. You don't want to do things that jeopardize that kind of thing, and you try to find things that everybody can deal with, that people just can't have an objection to, do you know what I mean? Not any kind of indoctrination, but just exposing a child to the whole idea of investigating things and coming to conclusions about certain things. That's my kind of approach to dealing with those kinds of things. You have to get acquainted with people, with their ideas. It may not be your particular way, but I just sit back and watch it. Each one of us has different ways, and when you are in classrooms with different teachers you can just sort of hear different things that they're doing, and you pick out the ones you like. You can learn a lot from the different ways other people do things.

Cynthia: Yes, that is true investigation, which you do a whole lot. What advice do you have for a person who has trouble doing that - an adult who is not used to investigating, exactly the way you've described it - watching very closely in order to learn and to relate constructively?

Brenda: It's really hard for me to say. The kind of person who doesn't do that kind of thing, they're in the habit of doing it differently, and it's very difficult to break habits and even think beyond that. But we have to, because the society and the world depend on people being able to put down these types of shortcomings and narrow ways of thinking. If a person doesn't want to do it, I think it would be much more difficult for them to transform themself, of course. But if a person wants to do it, I think he just has to consciously make the effort. It's something that comes from you, you know. Of course other people can help you.

If you are an adult around children, you wonder why they act the way they do. Look at yourself, and it's all there - they are a mirror image of you to a great extent. Myself, I'm really very conscious of not putting kids down. Even when children come to me with a problem I ask, "Well, what happened?" not making pre-judgments because a lot of times we are just *wrong*. We should avoid quick decisions about the kids getting into stuff, and making side comments which are often inconsiderate. It's really something to think about. You don't know what happened, and even after looking into it you still may not know because you don't have enough information. Children should be part of the decision-making when possible; however, you may have to explain that "Based on what I have heard, this is the way it's going to be." But I try to avoid pre-judgement, unless it's the type of situation which might require that, because kids can take advantage of any approach. I always try to offer explanations, so they can begin to understand what my reason is for making requests, because they have a lot of understanding. But you have to make a conscious effort with kids coming to you. One thing I do - when they have a problem, they have to bring the other party, dependent on the nature of what happened. A lot of times I just say, "Now look, this is something between you two - you two go and talk it over and resolve this". But a lot of times the kids will come to you, and you're down, and you say, "Why did you do this?" not "Did you do it?" That is subtle, but that is key number one of how you know something. When you talk to children, what tone of voice do you ask them in? Do you ask them in a way of putting them down or of doubting their word or showing that you don't have an open mind? You ask, "Did you see it yourself?" really trying to find out. Wherever I go I try to put these kinds of things into practice. In schools, especially the larger ones, it is really difficult to. There is all this gang fighting and stuff going on. I think one of the really important things a teacher must do is bring the kids together, any kind of way you can think of, and talk about it. I mean, it's a hard, long process, because after all you are dealing with what they have to survive on the streets. But we just have to begin somewhere to bring down hostile relationships and begin to build constructive ones.

This second interview is with Herbert Kohl, who is teaching kindergarden-first grade at Hillside Primary, a Berkeley public school. Mr Kohl is also teaching student teachers who are enrolled is an elementary credential programme at the University Without Walls-Berkeley. Prior to teaching kindergarten-first grade, Mr Kohl was principal of one of the first alternative junior-senior high schools in Berkeley. He has also taught fourth through sixth grades in the Harlem area of New York City. In between teaching Mr Kohl is a writer: *36 Children* (1967), *The Open Classroom* (1969), *Teaching the Unteachable* (1967), *Anthony Cool as Golden Boy* (1972), *Reading: How To* (1973), *Half the House* (1974), and *Math, Writing and Games in the Open Classroom* (1974).

AN INTERVIEW WITH HERBERT KOHL

Herb: It seems to me that there are two things that one can look at in terms of how Freire is used. One is how his specific literacy techniques can be used or modified, and two, how some of the ideas that he has can be incorporated into different programmes. Those are not necessarily the same. Given the notion of understanding and coming to a realization of the validity of one's culture and one's voice, that is, to realize that one's everyday actions have to do with culture, and that it is possible through a strong sense of one's own creative input into the world to take increasing power over oppressive conditions - that can be dealt with in a lot of different ways. I take that to be one of his central theses. I think a lot of that, for example, can be dealt with in terms of the kind of ethnic primers that we are making, which are not particularly radical in terms of any pedagogical ideas, but in terms of the very, very strong sense of everyday culture, the very, very strong senses of images not of the oppressor but of images of oneself.* It is just a whole way of transferring the material, the style, the context, the very definition of what is worth learning. That becomes one important way of dealing with some of his more general ideas - the whole question of what is of value is what the majority culture says is of value. So even though you learn things, and as you're learning things from your relatives and your parents, and things are being transferred to you, you don't value them. Or you have an ambiguous relationship

*The Centre for Open Learning and Teaching has developed, through a grant from the Dolores Kohl Educational Foundation, four bilingual primers for Spanish-speaking children in this country. The primers were written and illustrated by Chicano writers and artists.

towards the valuing of them. When that is shifted to the point of valuing them, you have a transvaluation, a real change of values, in which some of the materials of the oppressor can be incorporated into your system, as opposed to incorporating yourself into the system of the oppressor.

That can be done in a lot of different ways, and literacy is not the only vehicle necessary for that. Music, theatre, dance, games, just language, even oral language, the validity of one's own oral language, and the re-translation . . . I've noticed, for example, a lot of black kids beginning to understand how to read history books, how to translate history books written for the validation of white capitalist culture into terms of oppressing other people rather than trying to help other people in a liberal way. They have to re-translate words like progress and discovery and therefore understand that language, certainly the language of history and the language of self-justification, is moral and not objective description of the world. A lot of that has to do with understanding notions like justice, notions like equality. When people come to an awareness that language is being used to confound them and can be re-translated into language which is both their own and much clearer-headed, you have a form of liberation. You have a real form of pedagogy, I mean, that is teaching and learning.

I think also, for example, with children as opposed to adults, it is possible to start with a different set of values, especially young children. A certain amount of de-education, of decontamination or re-valuation is necessary, but often just by presenting things as being valid, by presenting a different vision of history, you don't have to discover that the vision that was imposed upon you is wrong, you discover a different vision to start with. That's the difference between undoing oppression of people totally convinced by oppression and educating for non-oppression, educating to govern, as people in Detroit call it.*

In terms of Freire's literacy - *how* it is being used I really don't know. I think one way that some of it is being used, whether it comes from Freire or not is irrelevant, is the idea that every single community, and of course on a basic level you can get down to every single child but this is on a more political and general level, ought to build its own programme for the teaching of reading, based on what is most familiar and what is of greatest value within that community. Community can be defined very narrowly in terms of just a small neighbourhood or a section of a barrio, or it can

**Education to Govern: A Philosophy and Program for Learning Now*, published by the All-African Peoples Union. Copies are available for 75c from: Advocators, Box 07249, Gratiot Station, Detroit, Michigan 48207.

be defined in terms of a locality. Probably as Freire says, the more general it gets, the less impact it tends to have on the people who are learning. Certainly there is no reason why the stuff that Freire uses with adults can't be used as the very basis upon which to begin to teach reading to young children. You know, the idea that you go into the community, and you analyze not only what words and concepts are visually present but what ideas and - relationships are of most interest and are most charged. The kids, of course, will be able to build on those as a way of doing things.

Another idea which I think is crucial to Freire and others, which I don't see people talking about enough, is discussion, discourse, what he calls dialogue. You don't just teach reading, and you don't just teach words, but you start by talking about yourself and your culture, you start by talking about conditions and circumstances of the world you live in, and you end up by talking about language. So you don't just learn the language, but you actually think about it, you discourse about it, you talk about the way words come together. For example, in schools we tend to train kids, to put kids through a series of exercises. Sometimes I find myself doing it, just being completely conditioned to it - things like top, tap, tep, whatever you like. We don't say to the kids that words come together in this way, that when you have three letters there is a sound at the beginning and a sound at the end, that you can change the languauge, that you can make these discoveries. We don't educate the kids to have a kind of meta-awareness about learning to deal with language in print. Freire spends a lot of time on that, as I understand the way he presented the thing - a lot of time having people think about 'Oh, look at those words,' or 'Look how they come together', exploring combinations that do and don't make sense, the same way in which they start exploring their own environment. And I think the implications are very great. It is possible even on, I think, the level of 5 year olds and 6 year olds that you can talk about language. You can actually have children begin on some conscious level to analyze the way in which reading and writing work. Even in English. Analyze exceptions and do a little bit of historical analysis of why so many exceptions exist.

Cynthia: We talked once about how for adults this kind of analysis can happen rather quickly, because of their adultness, their experience - and that for children it doesn't happen so rapidly.

Herb: Yes, I would put a lot more emphasis for kids on writing than on just the reading act. Freire doesn't do that, so far as I know. But the real pin-pointing and thinking about language - one's own language and other people's language - seems to come both in the act of writing and in the creation of stories, in the making of language of one's own and then recording it and sharing it with other people. On a day by day basis that is where a lot of the reinforcement and the familiarity gets in. That's where the questions arise. How does this go together? Does it go together? That's where I've seen a lot of creative phonics in our class, in the sense of kids trying to make some intelligent guesses as to how something should be transcribed, once they understand something about the nature of the language. I would do a lot of that.

The kids frequently need focus when they do writing. The intelligence with which you chose the themes to focus them on, to help them, has to do with how excited they become, and how involved they become in the language. But it also is a very strong force for teaching itself. For example, we've been doing a lot of stuff on superheroes. The reason is, first of all, superheroes are present in the kids' environment every day, both in their fantasies and on television and in the movies they see and the characters they act out on the streets. Superheroes at the same time represent archetypal forms of models that the kids either have or don't have. We've really had an opportunity to talk about, for example, why models for white middle class males are so dominant in this cutlure. With very young children you can't discuss something once, and with anybody you don't preach or give something once and for all. Young kids love repetition much more than adults, and they love the notion of variations on a theme. I've seen over and over again the theme developing. The kids will add something to it, or take away something, or change it in one way or another. They love to hear the same story over and over again and look at the same pictures. Those give an opportunity, not just for one but for many, many discussions, many, many coming back to the whole question. For instance, our class discussed superheroes - Black and Chicano superheroes, female superheroes, who are the people who make up the superheroes, what are their possibilities. All of these things involve the kids then discovering that they, too, or people that they can identify with in their fantasies, can be their own superheroes. They can be their own gods, in effect, as opposed to having to accept a dominant culture's white male dominance as the strong and the powerful, the omniscient and omnipotent.

Cynthia: In your thinking this year what are the things you have found are most powerful for the kids. You have mentioned superheroes. What other ones?

Herb: The power of mind over the power of brute force - that is why Anansi is so wonderful, because Anansi uses intelligence as opposed to physical strength to outwit people. That idea appears throughout the entire Ashanti culture. One of the big stools consists of an antelope standing on the back of an elephant, and the proverb that goes with that is "One gets to the top through guile, through brains, rather than through mere brute strength." That also, by the way, has an immediate, other identity which is why the Anansi stories we've been using are so good. If it is guile and intelligence as opposed to brute strength, then the young people can also understand that they can manage adults, children can save and help adults and have the intelligence to deal with adult things. The only thing the adult might have - they might have some wisdom too - but the only thing many adults have on kids is the fact that they are bigger.

Another theme is power, and that we dealt with in terms of actual electricity and magnetism, where power is located and how it can be controlled, getting power out of a battery and lighting up a bulb, one's own physical force and strength and how that can be used, controlled, utilized. The whole question of self-control and the utilization of one's own resources is substantiated in very concrete form in the day by day playing with bells and batteries and then talking about it and getting from there to the notion of storage of power and utilization of power.

Let's see what else. Oh yes, monsters and beasts - deformity - what's beautiful and what's ugly is another theme. You see all of those things have to do with who controls who and who oppresses who and things of that sort. The theme of light, illumination, that has to do with understanding, identifying things, of clarity. Let's see - other themes: mapping, again locating oneself in space, in time, in the world, in the universe. Mapping has the other part of it, which is really the central theme, which is mobility. The ability to find one's way home, the ability to go from one place to another, the ability to be mobile in the world. Then we get into the whole study of boundaries, where one can and can't go and why one can't go there. Then the question arises of how boundaries come up and who imposes boundaries. Those would be about the central themes that we have had so far.

Cynthia: How have you dealt with the linguistic part of Freire's approach? Have you tried to analyze the English language in any thorough, comprehensive linguistic way?

Herb: I haven't found it necessary. The only thing I did with Freire is use, at the beginning of the school year, each kid's name and the letters in their names to make up as many different words as possible and try to build a personal grammar. But I've found with kids you don't have to really give them all the linguistic concepts right away. It doesn't seem necessary at all. What you have to give them is very interesting stories written on a simple level, trust that they have the intelligence to make generalizations and leaps after a lot of exposure, and when kids are having trouble be on top of it enough to know how to reinforce it. Through their own names I've given the kids some general notion of transformation of letters, of changes of vowels and consonant sounds, on a very personal level they can remember. I've mostly worked with stories and books and just lots of reading of books and lots of reinforcement of books, and the kids' own writing. I haven't found a need to have a generative vocabulary. I could have done it, but it just didn't seem necessary, and it seemed a waste of time. I would do that generative vocabulary if I were working with older kids who had had major experiences of failure within their own lives and in school. In other words, I would try to do a generative vocabulary of the kids' own world, start with those words and show them how to work on those words to build a series of constructs of other words and use them to help deal with unfamiliar language.

Cynthia: Can you describe why it would be helpful to do that with older kids who have a history of failure?

Herb: Because they need something really familiar to start with and really charged - and they are afraid of books. Young kids are just absolutely fascinated by books. They're just magical and filled with all kinds of wonderful things. Older kids, if you give them simple books, have such a moral feeling about their being baby books, or being books that prove them inferior, a whole series of moral associations, you know. But very few of the really small kids have that feeling. Though I would say third graders begin to have that feeling about themselves as readers. They have experienced four years of failure in school by the end of the third year. You've got to realize they are probably eight years old, and at that point half their lives they've been reading failures. By that time, in the fourth grade, I'd start *all* over again, I really would.

The other thing that is nice about Freire's kind of analyzed, generative central vocabulary is that it randomizes the kid's experience. They never have experienced that way of approaching language before. What kids need who have failed is not more of the same, but a randomization so that they are dealing with the thing in an entirely new manner. People who have failed also very much need being able to talk about their own situation. They need to know that they are not failures, and the whole point of Freire's analysis that could help in that context is leading kids to the sense that they are not failures, but that the system has failed them in some way, that therefore they have the capacity to read, to do all these things. The vocabulary has got to be chosen, and it should not be just the school, not just an obsessive discussion of the school, but of all the really positive things that the kids do. In other words, it should be a validation as well as an analysis of their culture and of their learning and of their knowledge. You can see that dialogue is what the kids desperately need, especially kids who tend to be failures. The only talking they ever have at school or in a learning context is defiant, you know, telling the teacher to go somewhere or being wrong. I found this when I was teaching in Harlem, that the kids had all these pent-up things they wanted to say - about the world, about what they perceived about themselves, and they had never had any opportunity in their 6, 7, in some cases 8 years of schooling to do it.

Cynthia: That is also true about first and second graders, but maybe they don't have so much difficulty talking about it, because it's not yet in complete defiance of the school.

Herb: That's right. But in some cases in schools I've seen the first graders are really put in that context where they don't have much opportunity to talk because their time is always filled up with this activity and filling out these things. I know a first grader at Hillside, for example, who spends his entire day in school filling out work sheets. He told me he's the second best student in class, and his mother is delighted, and he's having a very hard time.

Cynthia: One other set of questions I have is about how you deal with the fact that there is more than one kind of English spoken by the children in our schools.

Herb: I find kids tend not to be that different from each other. Anyhow, that doesn't bother me, because I find kids able to deal in the most flexible way imaginable with the entire business of there being a similar code with slight differences in pronunciation. I guess I find it a made-up problem. When kids have really deep dialect problems, you adjust the way you write the language or you talk a lot more with the kids and let them listen. But anyone in America, who has been exposed to so much TV and exposed to so much of the standard language, has at least some minimal functional understanding of standard code.

Cythia: For instance, if you have a child who is telling you a story and you're transcribing it, do you transcribe it precisely the way they speak it?

Herb: Sometimes. What I tend to do is ask questions about it. I essentially say to the kid, 'Do you want me to do it this way or do you want me to do it this way?' Like, 'I might say it this way, and you might say it this way. Listen, which one sounds best to you? How do you want the other kids to read it?' And so instead of making it 'There's a proper way to do it,' I give the kids a choice. What I'm trying to do is educate their ear, give them a sense of language. As a writer I make those choices all the time. I must say a thousand times in every book that I've ever written I've had to make a choice as to what sounds right and what doesn't sound right, and who do I want it to sound right to. For example, I emphasize very, very strongly that I don't want my work to sound professionalized, academized, and therefore I spend a lot of time cutting out excess adjectives. Other people really believe that they want to lend a kind of academic authority to their work, so they bloat the language a little bit. Those are, in some cases of bad writers, not conscious choices. But with a lot of professional writers those are absolutely conscious choices one makes as to how to go about doing things. I would like the kids to have those choices too. The other thing the kids might know is that sometimes you use one and sometimes you use the other. For example, there is a difference in some telling in which dialogue is done in one way and descriptive language is done in another. For example, the dialogue might be much closer to vernacular speech to represent a range and variety of dialect, whereas the descriptive part might be a little more standard. On the other hand, it depends on who the narrator is, who is talking, who he is talking to, and who the audience is as well. I mean not only who he is talking to in the book but who is he talking to as an audience of the book - the reader. But that's really getting the kids to understand something about language as a creative act. I like to put the kids in the situation continually of making those choices themselves.

Cynthia: You have been describing ways that you have thought about Freire in the context of a first grade classroom. Have you been working in any other context that seems related?

Herb: One thing is working with young children in trying to develop some sense of conscientization - a sense of their own power, a sense of who they are and what they can do. Much closer to the original intent of Freire, I think, and effective in some communities - I don't know how it would work in Berkeley - is the notion of working with parents of children, and in a sense shifting the notion of who is oppressed from the notion of the parents' being oppressed to the notion of their children being oppressed - that their children are not inferior but oppressed and that they themselves can contribute to undoing the oppression of their children. I found that an extremely powerful way to mobilize a community, to get individual people re-thinking their own lives through re-conceiving what their children can do. I'll tell you what I mean by that. It is a very dramatic, in a sense a very awful thing to witness - parents whose children have failed in schools in which, and this is what's important, most of the children are failing. Parents as a group feel that their children are inferior. And the teachers perpetrate that idea, and the administration perpetrates that idea; Moynihan perpetrates that idea, Coleman perpetrates that idea, Jensen perpetrates that idea, Nixon . . . I mean there is a whole weight coming down on parents' feeling that their children simply can't do it. The parents therefore look for the gifted child who can make it as an escape, as opposed to looking to all of their children or analyzing the institution. So you start with a really classical condition of oppression, where the oppressed believe in their own oppression, see their own children being oppressed, and feel guilty about it but feel powerless to do anything about it because they believe it is somehow innate to their children. They are totally unable therefore to analyze the institution. Therefore, the problem is to get parents to re-conceive the potentialities of their own children.

What you have to realize is that you can't simply do it on the basis of street skills or skills that the kids have around the home or skills that the kids have within the community, just exactly because of what Freire said - people don't believe that is real culture. They don't believe that is really of value, and therefore the fact that their children speak Spanish doesn't mean anything. The fact that their children can repair cars, the fact that their children can act with intelligence in all kinds of ways but not function in school just simply doesn't invalidate how school puts the children down. It is still the school's judgment that outweighs in every way the parents' conception of their children's ability to function. So there are several things that have to happen. One level, which is much more like Freire and which has to be done on an adult level, is really to get people to become aware of the fact that they do create culture, they do make culture, that in their own adult lives they can have the power if they take it. Another strategy, and I think the real thing we are looking for is strategies which will have an impact on communities, is to lead parents to re-conceive the intellectual functioning of their children and to understand that their children in fact can read, can write, can learn, can deal with the oppressors' culture on their own terms, can master it and overcome it, and that in effect their children are capable of functioning in an intellectual way, in a cognitive way - you know, all the words that people use in order to put the kids down.

Cynthia: Have you found any concrete, dramatic ways to show parents this?

Herb: That's precisely what I was trying to get at. One of the things that Ray and myself and a lot of other people at the Centre have done is spend a lot of time exploring games, exploring ways of using natural language to get at the ability to read in any language or in any dialect - natural meaning language that is produced by a person from their needs and interests and the language that surrounds them in their own everyday life. So we have come to things from the point of view of language, from the point of view of strategy games - games which require thought and which can be directly turned into mathematical games which can be directly turned into mathematical concepts and abstract concepts and scientific ideas which are very simple - having to do with the nature and distribution of power - things like electricity and light, which can be grasped very easily by young children but which are very much of a put-off to adults. For example, if you put a bulb or a battery and a wire in the hands of most people - I'll put it even more strongly, in terms of most women who have been taught not to be able to deal with technology, in other words, most mothers of children who are poor - they will not be able to do it. Now you put the same equipment into the hands of a young boy and a young girl five, six, or seven, and those children will be able to do it. And when the light lights up, the mother lights up. It is just extraordinary. From that point you can do things like tell the kids, would you do it again and again, and now would you draw a picture of what you did. The kids can actually draw a very accurate circuit diagram, and then we can label the picture and we can start reading. The parents watching their children do that, who have been told that their children are illiterate, they can't understand science, they can't command technology and all, see that somewhere they have been lied to. The same things comes when you give parents, and this is men and women, a very complicated puzzle - something like a tangram or some rather abstract design to put together or some strategy game like mankala or wari or Go or chess to play. The parents will simply not be able to do it. However, the children will do it right away, and the parents will say, 'Now you can't call that child stupid'.

That is a context, by the way, I don't think has been talked to much before, the context in which parents and children are together with somebody whose role is "political education", but really it is conscientization, somebody whose role isn't to preach so much but to talk or to show pictures or to do the stuff that Freire said, to present the children with materials to which the children could respond to and then show the parents how to watch their children. That is the real role I've been playing, actually pointing out to the parents, 'Look, look at what your child is doing'. For example, I've got a whole bunch of things that one can do with Cuisinaire rods, because that seems like real mathematics. I take simple things like little hand calculators with memories and show how fast the children understand how to use a hand calculator and a memory and how the parents themselves are afraid of the machines. I take all kinds of equipment - electrical equipment, lights, mirrors so the kids can deal with reversal of images and reflection and all kinds of things. And as the children are working it is terribly important to translate what the children are doing to the parents into terms that will make them understand how that relates to school experience. The other thing, for example, that I've done which is wonderful is with these little rubber stamps of animals and all kinds of creatures. Children stamp the stamps and then make comic books out of them by putting little balloons coming out of their mouths saying things. Children start writing stories when they are told they can write without any constraint on grammar and language and what language they write in and what dialect and all. As the parents see their children flower you simply have to let it happen for a while. Then you have to sit down with the parents after that and say, 'Let's look at what has really happened. The school says this, your child does this, the school says your child can't do this, you've seen your child do it. Now let's . . . ' That's where the Freire thing comes in. I don't draw the conclusion. What's happening? - that's the real question. What's happening here so that all of this occurs, and you have a concrete experience of something which is different. I think a lot of us ought to keep on spending a lot of effort in designing materials. First of all, the same thing we are designing is really what ought to be in our classrooms anyway, or in our schools or in our community-based operations or whatever, because that is the way children like to learn. But it is terribly important to educate the children's parents to know that treated well and given some attitude that wants them to have strength, and I think that is very crucial, that of course they are going to do it.

We have talked about how the parents feel about their children initially in schools, then about the parents re-conceiving how their children function and in a sense being shown and helped in terms of the coordinates that you give them and the experiences that you present that their children are not to blame for their children's failure. Then you get to the stage where you present a situation for analysis. The situation for analysis is the school. Who did it? Who is responsible? Where did it come from, since your child can do it? Now you have a real problem - how do you deal with getting parents to do an analysis of the school? I think that ought to be structured, and you have to do it, again as Freire so wisely said, on the basis of each individual community because you have got to look at the schools you are dealing with. You can't come into a community and do that and leave and expect that the parents will know. They have to know what to analyze. So what you have to do is find a way to get the school texts that exist. You have to find a way to set a series of questions, focuses, things for parents to look at that you might define as damaging to their children. If you have a group leader who knows something about schools you can start looking at the structure of the school, the expectations of the teachers, the materials the teachers use, the way in which children are grouped, how children are dealt with, how boys are dealt with, how girls are dealt with, the tone and nature of the school.

I'll give you an example. When I was in Texas recently - I mean this is really part of analysis, and parents who walked into the school saw but they didn't see. When you get into the school it said, 'Great Things Come From Children of Families Like Ours' - a big statement which is really very positive. There is a picture of George Washington and Abraham Lincoln and underneath them are two Anglo families - blonde, blue-eyed, wearing suits and ties, coming out of the suburbs of the Fifties or the Forties. Essentially what that says is that families like the ones on the bulletinboard are the ones who do great things, but your families in the school don't do anything. Now something like a bulletin-board like that is a subject for analysis. It tells everything you need to know about the school once you get people to look at it on the level of: What does this do to our children? Let me put myself in the light of my children and what does this tell me about myself? What does this tell me about my community? These are questions that parents constantly have to be able to ask when they walk into a classroom and look at the displays the teacher gives: the books and the pictures and the texts, the kind of materials that the children are presented with at every point. The parents have to ask: What does this tell my children about me, their mother or father? What does it tell them about where they live, and what does it tell them about what it is possible for them to do?

What I did, by the way, in the school is I said, 'I am outraged.' I said this to my friends, and I looked at the kids and said, 'Hey, does that look like your family?' The kids all said yes to start with. And I knew they were lying to me or that they were afraid to tell me the truth or that they were so oppressed that they saw themselves in terms of the mirror as Anglos - in terms of what they were supposed to say, because they didn't see themselves that way, that's the way they were supposed to see themselves. I finally said, 'Well, now let's really kind of look at it.' We started doing it. I asked a couple of teachers who were sympathetic to me, 'I would like pictures of Chicano families. Are there any in the school?' It took them two days to find one. Finally, they found two pictures, but you see they had to look for pictures of Chicano families because they weren't there. They were not present. Now that tells you, that is part of the analysis. The other thing I did was I cut out those families, and I pulled the other things off the bulletinboard, and I put up Chicano families. Now you come into the school, and it says: 'Great Things Come From Families Like Ours', and then you see pictures that really could come from the neighbourhood and families from the school. And I asked the kids, and the same thing with the parents: What does this tell you as opposed to what did the other one tell you? How is this different? At every point you have to be more than abstract, in the sense that when you see something like that, what you have to really ask the parents is: how do you change it? In other words, how do you create new culture? If you want the parents to understand their creative power, you actually have to encourage them to use that power and to become creative in re-doing the environment and then to spend a lot of time in the environment of the school.

Questions that you can ask parents when they come in to analyze the school: If you came in at night with no children here, who would you think were the children who attended here? What could the school tell you about the children? You learn there are some thoroughly outrageous things: in other words, that they are not their children. It wouldn't tell you anything about their children. You would think it was a suburban middle-class school, or you would think it was a penal institute. You can do this also with the parents on the level of a classroom by classroom analysis. Take the entire thing - the principal's office. Who greets you? How are you dealt with? What are the things up? What are the bulletin-boards? Read the materials that the teachers send to each other. Look at the documents. Look at the concerns. What you are doing is using the school, for the parents, as in a sense a mirror of the whole culture. A lot of people who aren't even particularly and specifically concerned with schools can use an analysis of the school to deal with an analysis of almost any hierarchical, bureaucratic institution of oppression in capitalist society because they have very, very similar structural characteristics and very similar characteristics in terms of their attitudes towards oppressed people.

At a certain point, when all of this happens, the institution starts responding to increased knowledge. This is a level on which Freire didn't last long enough - well, I mean Freire was a victim of that institutional response to conscientization. What really happens is that the institution begins to respond to that awareness in more overt ways, and that becomes a very crucial point. That is what we've been seeing in Texas and other places. The institution at that point simply starts outlawing parent participation, trying to intimidate people from looking too closely. The consequence of a real analysis of a school is often either minimal or co-opted change, but more often in places where there is real oppression and great confidence on the part of the oppressor, there is an attempt then to find victims and to intimidate one or two people. At that point the process of conscientization turns into the process of developing sensible political action, which is the same thing. It's a different level of the same process. But it's a whole additional component because at that point people have to be out there to take risks, and if they are really poor - You see, some very funny things happen. There are some people who'll say, as I've seen some people saying, 'Look, I'm so poor I don't really give a shit. I have nothing. You can't take nothing away from me.' Other people will say, 'I am marginal, and I might make it, and therefore I'm afraid.' So you have a whole new process of politics and conscientization. At that point you simply cannot do it as an outsider. If you are going to deal with a community that is going to take those risks, the person who is there has to have the same commitments, take the same risks, and be with them at the same time.

I think one of the main failures of a lot of political organizing in the United States is that one can bring people to that level of awareness, but then all of the people who are doing the organizing and the intellectual shit, when it gets really dangerous, leave. At that point it is absolutely crucial, if you are going to do something like this, to spend a long time training people from the community. Now how you do it, that is your business, and how you make contact with people you can trust who are willing to take those risks is another thing. But you can't do that without having people who are going to lead the struggle on an everyday level when it reaches the point of being an overt struggle for political power and for economic power. But I think it would be romantic to believe that conscientizaçǎo in Freire's terms itself leads to victory and changing of the condition of oppression. The case of Brazil shows that is simply not true. Conscientization changes the level and nature of struggle, but for a while makes it more dangerous. Therefore one has to really have strong leadership and people prepared to take risks and great intelligence in planning, in developing and devising of strategies. So the process keeps on going.

After Deschooling – What?
Ivan Illich
25p

Illich is the person who first publicised the term 'deschooling' particularly in his book 'Deschooling Society'. For him deschooling 'must be the secularization of teaching and learning'; its concern is 'personal growth'. It involves the disestablishment of schools, the building of an educational world: and 'a new approach to incidental or informal education'. But while he advocates this disestablishment, he is aware of the dangers it entails: 'If the school continues lose its educational and political legitimacy, while knowledge is still conceived as a commodity, we will certainly face the emergence of a therapeutic Big Brother' . . . 'Unless we guarantee that job relevance is the only acceptable criterion for employment, promotion, or access to tools, thus ruling out not only schools but all other ritual screening, then deschooling means driving out the devil with Beelzebub.'

Classrooms of Resistance
Chris Searle
Cloth edition £2.75
Paperback 85p

In a school in Poplar during the last two years, Chris Searle has been attempting to 'develop through imaginative writing, the generous, empathetic and fraternal instincts' of the children he teaches. The Chile coup, the South African miners' strike, Ulster, the Flixborough disaster, and nearer home, the opening of the £8,000,000 Tower Hotel on the site of the old St Katherine's dock, to mention but a few, are events which are discussed in the classroom. From these discussions come the children's poetry, prose and drama contained in this book. It is illustrated throughout with photographs and line drawings.
It is in the children's work that the ideology of Searle's teaching is powerfully revealed: he believes that Education is only valid if it contributes to liberating all mankind, and that his teaching must further 'the knowledge and resistance to, and organisation against exploitation and subjection, and contact and empathy with the oppressed of the world'.